GUINEA PIGS

GUINEA PIGS

by Elvig Hansen

A Carolrhoda Nature Watch Book

Carolrhoda Books, Inc./Minneapolis

Thanks to Bruce Nathanson, Petland, St. Louis Park, Minnesota, for his assistance with this book.

This book is available in two editions:
Library binding by Carolrhoda Books, Inc.
Soft cover by First Avenue Editions
c/o The Lerner Group
241 First Avenue North
Minneapolis, MN 55401

This edition first published 1992 by Carolrhoda Books, Inc.
Original edition copyright © 1988 by Kinderbuchverlag Reich
Luzern AG, Lucerne, Switzerland, under the title
LIEBENSWERTE MEERSCHWEINCHEN. Based on the
Danish manuscript MARSVINE-LIV.
German translation by Heidrun Flüeler. English translation by Amy Gelman.
Adapted by Carolrhoda Books, Inc.
All additional material supplied for this edition © 1992 by
Carolrhoda Books, Inc.

LIBRARY OF CONGRESS CATALOGING-IN-PUBLICATION DATA

Hansen, Elvig.
  [Marsvine-liv. English]
  Guinea pigs / by Elvig Hansen.
     p.   cm.
  Translation of: Marsvine-liv.
  "A Carolrhoda nature watch book."
  Includes index.
  Summary: Describes the physical characteristics, habitat, and
life cycle of the guinea pig.
  ISBN 0-87614-681-7 (lib. bdg.)
  ISBN 0-87614-613-2 (pbk.)
  1. Guinea pigs as pets — Juvenile literature. 2. Guinea
pigs — Juvenile literature. [1. Guinea pigs.] I. Title.
SF459.G9H36   1992   91-30694
636'.93234 — dc20

Manufactured in the United States of America
3 4 5 6 7 8 – P/JR – 01 00 99 98 97 96

People keep many kinds of animals as pets. Maybe you have a playful dog that likes to chase balls. Or a small, furry cat that sits on your lap and purrs when you stroke it. Some people keep pet birds because they enjoy their cheerful chirping. Others like fish, snakes, and lizards as pets because they stay in one place instead of roaming around your house.

The guinea pig is a pet animal that has some of the features of all these other pets. Guinea pigs are playful, and they like to be petted and held too. They squeak and squeal and make other interesting noises. And they are very happy living inside a cage in your house.

This book tells the story of some guinea pigs that live with the author and his family. It also explains what kind of animals guinea pigs are and what they have in common with their wild relatives.

When you first meet a guinea pig, you may be surprised to find that it doesn't fit its name. This small fur-covered creature with big bright eyes doesn't look much like a pig. In fact, guinea pigs are not in the pig family at all. They are **rodents**, related to hamsters, gerbils, mice, and squirrels.

The closest relatives of pet guinea pigs are the wild **cavies** (CAVE-ees) that live in parts of South America. These little animals make their homes in the mountains and grasslands of Peru, Bolivia, and other South American countries. Pet guinea pigs are descended from these wild rodents, and their official name is **cavy** too.

Long before Europeans first came to South America during the 1500s, Indians had tamed some of the wild cavies and were raising them for food. Spanish sailors probably brought the first cavies to Europe in the 1600s. No one really knows how they came to be called "pigs." It may have been because cavies were used as a food source in their homeland, just as pigs were in Europe. Another explanation for the name is that the rodents squeal and grunt and make other pig-like noises.

The "guinea" part of the guinea pig's name is also something of a mystery. Some people think that it may come from Guyana, a part of South America where cavies lived. Others claim that the word comes from "Guineaman." This was a name used for seafaring traders during the days when cavies were first brought to Europe. Another idea is that the first cavies sold in Europe cost a golden guinea coin.

Wherever they got their name, today guinea pigs are popular pet animals in many parts of the world. Now that you know something about the group, let's meet some real guinea pigs.

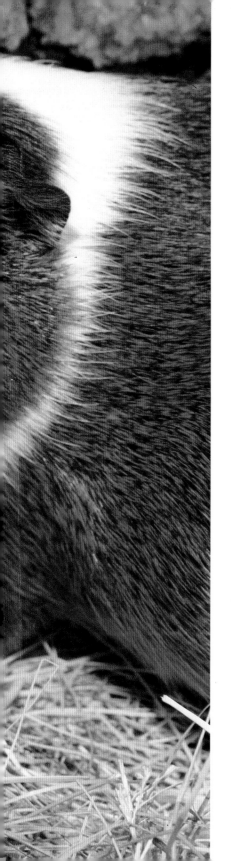

Here are Max and Maia, two of the guinea pigs that live with my family. Max (right) is a male. Like most male guinea pigs, he is larger than the female, Maia (left). Maia is also easy to recognize because she has one brown cheek and one reddish cheek.

About nine weeks ago, Max and Maia mated. Maia became pregnant, and now she is almost ready to give birth (below). During her pregnancy, Maia and Max stayed together. Unlike some other rodent mothers, Maia did not drive her mate away. Now, as the time of birth draws near, we have separated the two guinea pigs. This is so that they will not mate again right after Maia has her babies.

We want to see Maia's babies being born. But guinea pigs have their young quickly and without any fuss. We have to watch closely so that we can be with Maia at the right time.

We just looked in on Maia and found her peacefully nibbling hay in her cage. Now when we return a few minutes later, one baby guinea pig has already been born! There it is between Maia's legs.

About four minutes later, another baby guinea pig makes its appearance (upper left). The baby is enclosed in the **amniotic** (am-nee-AH-tik) **sac**, a transparent membrane that surrounded it while it developed inside Maia's body. Maia tears open the membrane with her teeth so that the baby can breathe (lower left). Then she eats the membrane.

Now Maia bites through the second baby's **umbilical** (um-BIL-ih-kuhl) **cord**. This lifeline connects the unborn baby to its mother's body. Now that the baby has been born, the cord is no longer needed. After eating the umbilical cord, Maia licks the little guinea pig clean (opposite). Although this is her first time as a mother, she knows exactly how to take care of her young.

After Maia finished cleaning up her second baby, we thought that a third young guinea pig was going to be born. Sometimes a female has three, four, or even five young at a time. But it was only the **placenta** (pluh-SENT-uh), or afterbirth, that was being pushed out of Maia's body (lower left).

The placenta is a structure that provided nourishment for the unborn baby. Now that its work is finished, Maia eats it as she did the amniotic sac and umbilical cord. Her **instinct** to do this comes from her wild ancestors. Mothers that give birth in the wild get rid of all the evidence so that other animals are not attracted by the smell. If **predators** (PRED-uh-tuhrs) know there are newborn young around, they might try to eat them.

Safe inside their cage, Maia's two babies don't have to worry about predators. After they have their first meal (opposite), they are ready to face the world.

Unlike some of their relatives, baby guinea pigs are fully developed at birth. When young hamsters and mice are born, they are hairless, blind, and completely helpless. But young guinea pigs have thick hair and good eyesight. They can move around soon after birth.

This difference in development is due to the **gestation** (jess-TAY-shun) **period** of the rodents. Baby hamsters grow inside their mothers' bodies for about 16 days. Guinea pigs have a much longer gestation period of about 63 days.

Maia's babies are only half an hour old, and they are already very active. Their little noses sniff the air and the hay as they explore their surroundings (left). One baby even begins to groom itself with its claws (above).

While her babies are getting acquainted with their world, Maia is ready for a meal. Giving birth was hard work, and now she needs to eat. She leaves the brooding corner of the cage and heads for a carrot on the opposite side. Her young follow close behind her (below). After Maia has eaten, she returns to the other side, with the little guinea pigs right at her heels (opposite).

This behavior is also inherited from the guinea pig's wild ancestors. In the wild, young guinea pigs have to stay with their mother for protection. When she goes away from the burrow, they go with her. Young pet guinea pigs also feel safest when they stick close to Mother.

Another reason that baby guinea pigs stay close to their mother is to get food. Like all young **mammals**, guinea pigs drink milk produced by their mothers' bodies.

Female dogs and cats have many **teats** (TEETS), or nipples, to feed their young, but female guinea pigs have only two. They are located on the stomach near the back legs. (The photograph below shows Maia's teats, which are two different colors.)

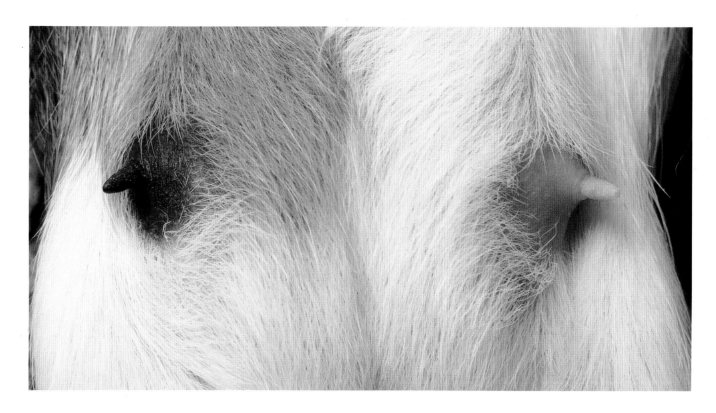

Like all young guinea pigs, Maia's babies nurse about every half hour. Maia sits to feed them. She doesn't lie down as some other animal mothers do. The babies sit too, squeezed in between their mother's front paws.

After the babies have nursed for two or three minutes, Maia stands up, taking their food away. The young guinea pigs follow her, asking for more. But Maia will decide when it is time for them to eat again.

Baby guinea pigs nurse for two or three weeks after they are born. But when they are several days old, they also start to eat solid food. At two days old, Maia's young started munching on carrots (below), greens, and hay. Two days later, they began eating grains and seeds (opposite).

We feed Maia and her family hay and a mixture of seeds and grains that we get at the pet store. You can also buy special guinea pig food that comes in the form of pellets. In addition to this dry food, we supply our guinea pigs with plenty of fresh foods like apples, carrots, and lettuce. They get fresh water every day in a bottle that attaches to the side of the cage. The guinea pigs can drink from the tube at the end of the bottle without spilling water.

After the young guinea pigs have eaten (opposite), they have another job to do. They have to get rid of their body wastes. Just as Maia feeds her babies and protects them, she also helps them to keep clean. When a young guinea pig has to eliminate wastes, it lies on its back and holds its hind legs in the air (right). Its mother licks off the baby's urine and **feces** (FEE-sees) and eats them.

This behavior might not seem very appealing to us, but it is practical. It keeps the young animals clean and their living space tidy. When the babies get older, they will use one corner of the cage as their "toilet," as adult guinea pigs do.

Cleanliness is very important to guinea pigs. If you have pet guinea pigs, you need to help them keep their cage clean. At least once a week, all the bedding material should be replaced. The "toilet corner" of the cage should be cleaned daily.

While they are young, guinea pigs are very active and playful. This is certainly true of Maia's babies, and my family and I enjoy watching them play.

Here are the two of them racing around the cage (above). They chase each other back and forth and around and around, having a great time. Maia sits quietly, watching her lively young.

The young guinea pigs also like to leap and tumble in their play. They kick their back legs like little horses and wiggle their rear ends. Sometimes they jump so fast and high that they turn head over heels in the air and land smack on their stomachs. The youngster in the pictures on the right seems to be doing a handstand.

The babies play these wild games two or three times a day. By the time they are two or three months old, the young guinea pigs won't be so playful. At that age, they won't be babies anymore. At eight months, they will be fully grown adults.

Even when they are adults, most guinea pigs still like to play hide and seek. They bury themselves under the hay inside their cage. This habit is another one inherited from their wild ancestors. In the wild, cavies often hide in tall grass to avoid being discovered by predators.

Even in the safety of their cage, our pet guinea pigs enjoy burrowing in hay. Of course, they also like to eat hay, and sometimes they eat all the hay we give them for hiding. Then they have to hide under the straw bedding in the "sleeping corner" of the cage.

Sleeping is one of the favorite activities of guinea pigs at any age. When Maia and her young sleep, they cuddle close together. In the wild, guinea pigs live in small groups. Domestic guinea pigs feel comfortable when they are close to each other.

Just like humans, guinea pigs usually sleep at night and are awake during the daytime hours. Also like some people,

Maia and her babies were napping when I took the picture below. But the soft clicking of the camera pulled them from their dreams. The young ones will soon fall asleep again. It will take a while for the watchful Maia to close her eyes.

The excellent hearing of guinea pigs helps them to be aware of danger. This is very important for wild guinea pigs. These little animals cannot defend themselves against predators that want to eat them. They can escape only by running and hiding.

they take naps during the day. These naps are short—about 10 minutes—and during them, the guinea pigs sleep lightly. The slightest noise will wake them up.

In addition to sharp hearing, guinea pigs have a good sense of smell. Their eyesight is good too, but they depend more on smell and hearing to tell them what is going on in the world.

A guinea pig's large, bright eyes are among its most noticeable features. The condition of the eyes can tell something about a guinea pig's health. If the eyes are cloudy or red instead of clear and bright, then the animal may be sick. Sometimes a guinea pig's eyes get irritated by pieces of straw or hay. If your pet guinea pig has eye problems, you may need to get help from a veterinarian.

Take a look inside a guinea pig's mouth, and you will see some other important features. Like all rodents, guinea pigs have four large front teeth that are used for cutting. These teeth continue to grow throughout a guinea pig's life. They are kept at the right length by gnawing on hard objects.

If pet guinea pigs are given carrots to eat, they can keep their teeth in good shape. A block of wood in the cage also provides something hard to gnaw on. If a guinea pig's front teeth get too long, then they should be trimmed by a vet.

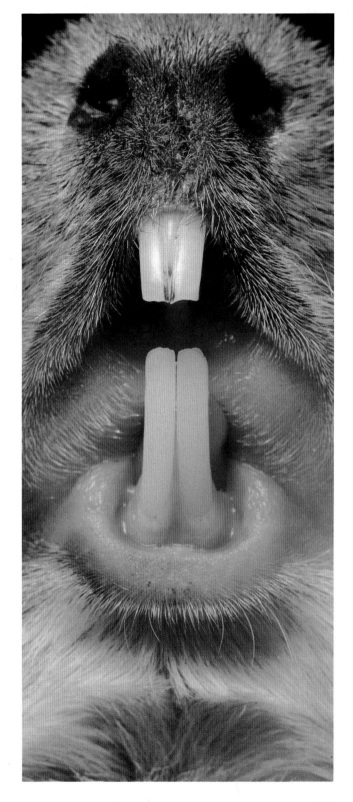

As we watch Maia and her new family eating and playing together, we are learning more about how guinea pigs communicate with each other.

Guinea pigs are noisy animals. They "talk" to each other with the sounds that they make. When it's time to nurse, Maia calls her young to her with deep grunting noises. When she plays with the babies, Maia murmurs to them softly and continuously. The young answer with a thin, gurgling sound.

If one young guinea pig gets too far away from Maia, it starts squeaking. It does not like to be separated from its family. The squeaking noise causes Maia to come looking for the baby. She nuzzles it and calms it with coos and gurgles.

Guinea pigs also "talk" to members of their human family. If one of our guinea pigs hears us approaching the cage, it pokes its head out of the hay and gives a loud squeak. This is its way of asking for food or for attention.

During the cold parts of the year, our guinea pigs live in wire cages inside our house. In summer, when the weather is warm, we move them outside.

When they are outdoors, the guinea pigs live in a **run**. This is a simple wood enclosure with a small box at one end to provide shade and a place to hide. The run doesn't have any floor but sits right on the ground. Unlike their wild relatives, domestic guinea pigs do not dig, so they will not try to burrow out of the run. They don't climb either, so they won't escape over the low walls.

We put a piece of wire mesh over the top of the run to keep other animals away from the guinea pigs. Without this protection, dogs or cats might attack them, or large birds carry them away.

In their outdoor run, the guinea pigs have plenty of natural food to eat. Grass, clover, dandelions—they munch on all these green plants. When they have eaten everything within the run, we simply move it to a different spot. We make sure, however, that the guinea pigs don't eat grass or plants that have been treated with chemicals.

Our guinea pigs enjoy their summer outdoors. It gives them a change of scene, a new diet, and plenty to do.

Our family owns quite a few guinea pigs, and some of them look very different from Maia and her young. Domestic guinea pigs come in many different colors. Even the length and texture of their hair can be quite different.

Some of the most popular pet guinea pigs have smooth or short hair. Maia, her mate, Max, and their young belong to this group. Smooth-haired guinea pigs are the easiest to take care of because they do not need a lot of grooming to keep their coats neat.

Guinea pigs with rough or long hair require more care, but they are very attractive. We have some rough-haired guinea pigs that belong to a group known as **Abyssinian** (ab-ih-SIN-ee-uhn). The hair of an "Aby" forms little whirls called **rosettes** (roh-ZETS) on various parts of its body. In the photo below, you can see an Abyssinian male (left) with a smooth-coated female.

The guinea pigs first brought from South America all looked pretty much alike. So where did all these different kinds of guinea pigs come from? They were developed by a process known as **selective breeding**. A breeder would look for guinea pigs with some unusual feature—for example, long hair. The mating of a long-haired male with a long-haired female might produce young with that same unusual feature. By continuing to mate long-haired animals to each other, a breeder could eventually create a whole new breed of guinea pigs with long hair.

Today, most breeders are not interested in creating new kinds of guinea pigs. They want baby guinea pigs that are **purebred**, with features just like all the others in their group. The best way of producing purebred animals is to choose two parents that have the same common features.

When we let our guinea pigs mate, my family is not so concerned about breeding. We like to see the combinations that result when we put different males and females together.

The photographs on the next page show one of our Abyssinian males getting ready to mate with a smooth-haired female. The male is **courting** several different females, trying to get one of them to accept him as a mate. Growling in a deep voice, he creeps up to a female and tries to touch her (top). If the female doesn't want to mate, she discourages the male by showing her teeth or kicking him with her back legs. She may even spray him with urine.

When a female is ready to mate, she lets the male approach her (below left). The mating itself (below right) lasts only a few seconds. About two months later, the female will give birth to some young guinea pigs. Since their parents had such different features, we are not sure what the young will look like.

In this picture, you can see the result of another mating between two different guinea pigs. The mother, shown here, is a rough-haired Abyssinian with a coat of only one color. Her mate is a smooth-haired male with three colors in his coat.

The four babies have different combinations of their parents' features. Some have smooth hair, while others have little rosettes like their rough-haired mother. Their colors are really varied.

We think that these baby guinea pigs are very unusual and attractive. It doesn't matter to us that they are not purebred.

The guinea pigs shown on this page are two pure-bred kinds sold by many breeders. At the top is a smooth-haired animal with a coloring that is known as **agouti** (uh-GOOT-ee). Each of its hairs has a mixture of two different colors. This kind of guinea pig looks a lot like the wild cavies of South America.

The guinea pig shown in the bottom picture is a long-haired **Peruvian** (puh-RUV-ee-uhn). Its thick, soft hair continues to grow throughout its life. As it gets longer, it will hang down all around the guinea pig's body, even over its face.

The Peruvian is popular with people who like to enter their guinea pigs in pet shows. To keep the animal's long hair in good shape, the owner will often tie it up in paper wrappers. When it is time for the Peruvian to go to a pet show, the owner takes off the wrappers and combs out the hair.

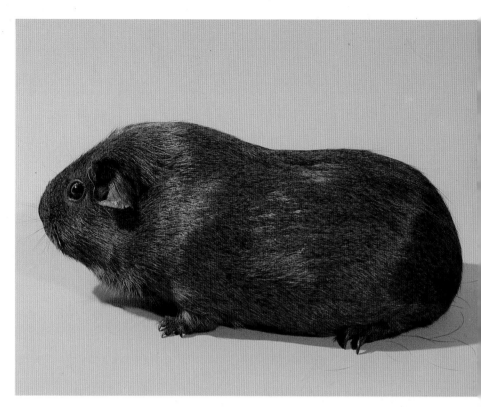

Here are three more unusual guinea pig breeds. One is a smooth-haired **satin** guinea pig (opposite above), named for its shiny coat. Also shown are two **crested** guinea pigs (opposite below). These funny little animals have smooth hair on most of their bodies, except for their heads. Between their ears, they have a single rosette that forms a kind of crest. Many crested guinea pigs have white rosettes with solid red bodies.

The **teddy** guinea pig (above) looks something like a fuzzy teddy bear. Its coarse hair is short—only about 1/2 inch (1.4 centimeters) in length—and stands up all over its body.

The teddy and the satin are two of the newer breeds of guinea pigs. Both were developed from the smooth-haired guinea pig in the 1970s. Sometimes these new breeds become popular as pets or for showing. Guinea pigs that are entered in shows, however, have to belong to breeds that are recognized by associations of guinea pig breeders. It usually takes a while for new breeds like the teddy to be allowed to compete for prizes in guinea pig shows.

Even if you have never been to a guinea pig show or seen a real guinea pig, the name "guinea pig" is probably familiar to you. You will often hear it used to describe a person who is the subject of a test or experiment.

For many years, real guinea pigs have served as test subjects in scientific laboratories. Like mice, rats, and hamsters, the little rodents have helped scientists to discover new medicines and cures for diseases. Many guinea pigs have given up their lives so that humans could have longer, healthier lives.

Both as pets and as test animals, guinea pigs do a lot for people. They deserve the care and love we give them.

GLOSSARY

Abyssinian: a breed of guinea pig with rough hair that grows in little whirls, or rosettes

agouti: a variety of guinea pig with fur in which each individual hair has two different colors. Many of the wild cavies in South America have this coloring.

amniotic sac: a thin membrane that surrounds an unborn animal inside its mother's body

cavy: the name for a guinea pig usually used by scientists and breeders. Guinea pigs belong to a scientific group called *Cavia.*

courting: choosing a mate and getting ready for mating. Guinea pigs and many other animals behave in special ways during courtship.

crested: a breed of guinea pig with a single rosette, or crest, of hair on the head

feces: solid waste materials passed out of an animal's body

gestation period: the period of time during which an unborn animal develops inside its mother's body

instinct: an ability or behavior that is inherited rather than learned

mammals: warm-blooded animals that nourish their young with milk produced by the mother's body

Peruvian: a breed of guinea pig with long hair that continues to grow throughout the animal's life

placenta: a structure that provides nourishment to an unborn mammal inside its mother's body. The placenta is also known as the afterbirth because it comes out of the mother's body after the baby is born.

predators: animals that hunt and eat other animals

purebred: having ancestors that belong to the same breed or type

rodent: a mammal that has large front teeth used for gnawing. Rats, squirrels, beavers, hamsters, and guinea pigs are all rodents.

rosettes: whirls or circles of hair in the fur of Abyssinian and other rough-haired guinea pigs

run: a large enclosure in which guinea pigs live when they are outside. Guinea pig runs usually have walls and a covering on top but no floor.

satin: a kind of guinea pig with very shiny hair. The smooth-haired satin is the most common, but breeders have also developed Abyssinian and Peruvian guinea pigs with satin coats.

selective breeding: choosing animals for mating in order to produce young

with special features, for example, long hair. Different guinea pig breeds were produced through this method.

teats: the nipples from which young mammals suck their mothers' milk

teddy: a breed of guinea pig with short, fuzzy hair

umbilical cord: a cord that connects an unborn mammal to the placenta. The baby receives nourishment through this "lifeline" while it is developing in its mother's body.

INDEX

ABOUT THE AUTHOR/ PHOTOGRAPHER

Elvig Hansen is one of the leading wildlife photographers in Denmark, where he makes his home. His pictures have appeared in books for both adults and children. In 1983, Mr. Hansen was awarded the Danish School Libraries' Children's Books Prize. Many of his books for young people are about animals. In addition to guinea pigs, he has produced books about toads, geese, goats, tortoises, and parakeets. Elvig Hansen knows a lot about guinea pigs because his family raises them. They started with only two guinea pigs in a cage, but they soon had many more.